FIRST GRADE FIQH

For Children , Beginners, and new Muslims

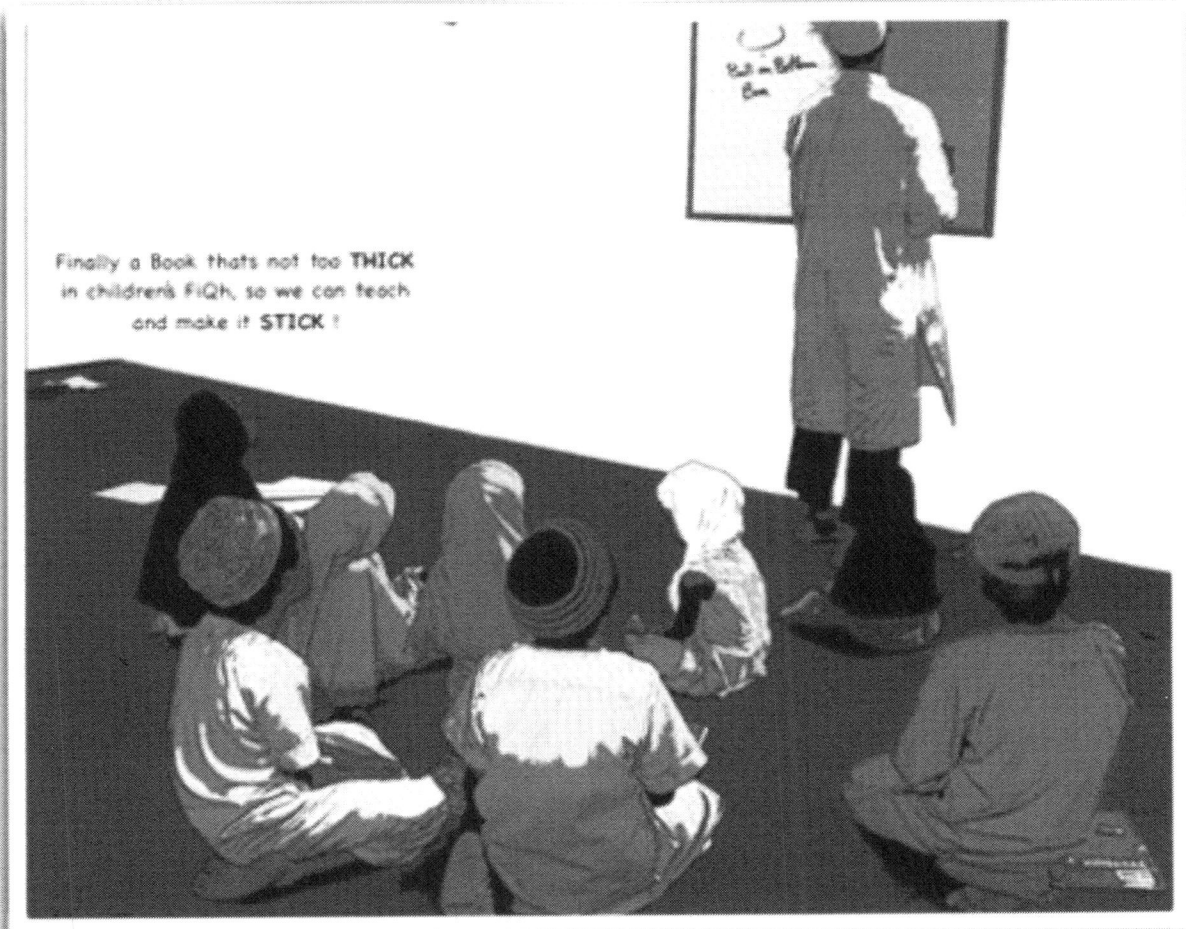

Finally a Book thats not too THICK in childrens FiQh, so we can teach and make it STICK !

By: Abu Taubah

MW01527972

Preface

In every islaamic culture there is a fiQh text that serves as a beginner's primer for children. These primers are usually in Arabic and/or the native language of that society. Due to the fact that we Westerner- Muslims were for the most part converts and new to islam, we tried to utilize the beginner books of fiQh that had been in use for hundreds of years in the lands of the Muslims. However, due to societal and linguistic differences, the texts from nonwestern cultures were often so difficult to understand that most of us stopped using them.

In the absence of any alternatives, the majority of us never became competent in fiQh; never changed many of the habits we had before islaam, hence why it has taken so long for many of us to develop islaamically and why some of us even fell back into kufr. It is also why we are not confident that we know all the fiQh that we are supposed to know. And furthermore, due to our lack of fiQh, why we didn't understand the important solutional-role fiQh played in the everyday life of the believer.

That is, until we had children. As time passed, and although slowly we continued to grow, we began to notice that our children were not developing their islaamic fiQh. At least, not as much or as quickly as they were picking up un-islaamic Western habits and mentalities. It was then that we realized the importance of fiQh for children.

With this in mind – We've spent our time

Praying hard – to make this rhyme

In children's FiQh – and not too thick

So we can learn – and make it stick

Apologies to those that write – and don't believe that rhyming's right

Allaah we'll ask – for me and you

To keep us all – upon the truth

I hope you all benefit from what I have presented. It is written in light of the pressing need to produce an appropriate text and technique for the use in developing the fiQh… in both parent and child.

abu taubah

MuHarram 1430 / January 2009

walHamdulillaah

Introduction

Bismillaahir RaHmaanir RaHeem

1. I gave my word with heart and head

2. To praise Allaah till I drop dead

3. Send blessings on the prophet and

4. Respect the scholars Ijtihaad

5. As muslims we must study and pray

6. To fight shayTaan in every way

7. We'll make mistakes along the way

8. Repent to fight another day

Chapter One

Understanding That
I am Responsible

9. So the first thing that I have to do

10. Now that I'm mukallafoon

11. Accountable in every way

12. My actions call on me to blame

13. Is look to see what faith demands

14. Have I complied with it's commands

15. What do I think about Allaah

16. Why it's correct and what's a flaw

NOTES

Chapter Two

The First Part of the Shahaadah

17. The meaning of **shahaadah** is the first thing we must know

18. There is no God for real that is except the One and only

19. The **KhalQu** He created it and for them He provides

20. He manages affairs of theirs from high above the sky

21. Too high I say sublime is He

22. For partners or **Nadheer**

23. And this is what **Shahaadah** means but let us make it clear

24. There are conditions tied to it to which we must adhere

25. There's knowledge , then **YaQeen** and then acceptance my sweet dear

26. Then **inQiyaadu** then there's **SidQ**, **IkhlaaSu** and **MaHabbah**

27. Allah we ask for help and to admit us into Jannah.

NOTES

Chapter Three

The Second part of The Shahaadah

28. Then every Muslim must concur

29. Muhammad is the Messenger

30. Sent by Allaah therefore we trust

31. Everything he said to us

32. We must obey his orders and

33. Respect the things he called **Haraam**

34. He brought the laws full and complete

35. Not one detail did he delete

36. All sacred laws must come from him

37. Salla 'alayhee wa sallam

NOTES

Chapter Four

The Five Main Acts of 'Ibaadah

38. And then I have to learn the things

39. I need to do my **farDu** **'aynz**

40. Like regulations of **Salaah**

41. And just how much to pay **Zakaah**

42. The parts of **Hajj** I have to do

43. It's **RamaDHaan** and I've the flu

44. This obligates all Muslimeen

45. To learn the laws and what they mean.

NOTES

Chapter Five

Why & How to Repent

46. I've sworn to do Allaah's command

47. And not to do one thing **Haraam**

48. So when I fail I must repent

49. Before I get a punishment

50. From up above Allaah most high

51. Before my soul is caused to die

52. Repentance will not be correct

53. Until I'm sad and feel regret

54. For what I've done and I intend

55. Not to do that sin again

56. And if still sinning I must stop

57. All sinful deeds right on the spot

58. And no it's not **Halaal** to say

59. I will repent MAYBE one day

60. For those who think like that will find

61. A devil has possessed their mind

62. He plans to drop their soul in hell

63. Turn to Allaah to break his spell

64. Say **Astaghfirullaaha wa atoobu ilayh**

65. A hundred times in every day

66. **Astaghfirullaaha wa atoobu ilayh**

67. That's all a Muslim has to say

NOTES

Chapter Six

WuDoo

68. Say **Bismillaah** and wash my hands

69. Once or twice or three times and

70. Wash my mouth and blow my nose

71. Then wash my face that's how it goes

72. I'll wash my arms until they bend

73. Then wipe my head and back again

74. Wash my ears inside and out

75. Go up and down till there's no doubt

76. Then make sure that I wash my feet

77. With ankles washed **wudooz** complete

NOTES

Chapter Seven

The FarDus Salaah

78. The **niyyaz** made before Salaah

79. Clear in my head made in my heart

80. **Takbeeratun** and all's **Haraam**

81. And we must try our best **Qiyaam**

82. Say **Hamdalah** and then **rukoo**

83. Then rise again we have to do

84. Twice on my face and sit between

85. **Tashaahud** comes before **tasleem**

86. With '**Itidaal** and **ITma'een**

87. And don't forget the right **tarteeb**

88. If we forget one **farD** that's all

89. The whole **Salaah** is null and void

NOTES

Chapter Eight

Seventeen Salaah

90. I wake up and I have to pray

91. Two **rakaa** to start the day

92. Before the sun rise **Fajr's** prayed

93. Afterwards **Duhaa** is claimed

94. Prayed **Istikhaarah** on the spot

95. Before I work the plans I plot

96. And when the sun gets passed midday

97. I'll offer **Zhuhr** without delay

98. Or **Juma** but that's once a week

99. Like **Eed Salaah** it's short and sweet

100. It hadn't rained for weeks and weeks

101. Prayed **IstisQaa** now my roof leaks

102. At 'Asr I'll be **Qaaniteen**

103. Save both my **dunyaa** and my **deen**

104. I tried to fix that leaky roof

105. The sun eclipsed I prayed **Khusoof**

106. **Mujaahidoon** march by my house

107. "In battle pray **Salaatul Khawf** "!

108. "Pray **Tawbah**..." one replied and said ,

109. "...When bad deeds hurt your heart and head"

110. Pray **Maghrib** and stay wide awake

111. So **Ishaa's** not missed by mistake

112. Then stand at night **Qiyaamul Layl**

113. With **Witr** and you'll never fail

114. **Janaazah** will be much too late

115. To pray **Salaah** I didn't make

NOTES

NOTES

Chapter Nine

RamaDhaan

116. When doors in **Jannah** open wide

117. And hell is locked devils inside

118. When **Shabaan** month strikes twenty-nine

119. The Muslims search the skies to find

120. The **RamaDhaan** new moons approach

121. With **taQwa** blessings and good hope

122. So if they sight the moon we fast

123. And when it's cloudy thirty pass

124. From **Shabaan** before **Ramadhaan**

125. The month of fasting and **Quraan**

126. The month we pray the **Taraweeh**

127. And wake up early if we sleep

128. The **Sunnah** is to eat and drink

129. A light **Suhoor** 'fore **fajrs** brink

130. And then from sunrise till it sets

131. We fast and leave all nourishment

132. It's what strong Muslims have to do

133. Obligating me and you

134. To intend the night before

135. A day of fasting for your Lord

136. But for the travelers and the sick

137. This obligation doesn't stick

138. And girls when menses come your way

139. You must stop fasting right away

140. And those who make themselves throw up

141. Or sneak and eat they should grow up

142. 'Cause those are two dumb dirty tricks

143. That break a fast you'll have to fix

144. Allah don't need us not to eat

145. If we still lie and act like creeps

146. When we fast we're generous

147. We read **Quraan** and we don't rush

148. So when you're fasting play it cool

149. And don't reply to every fool

150. But if someone disturbs your vibe

151. I'm fasting twice is our reply

152. Remember not to sleep all day

153. Or talk a lot with too much play

154. Then soon as we can't see the sun

155. From way up high our fast is done

156. The devil loses and we win

157. "Oh Allaah forgive our sin

158. The thirst is gone, the veins are wet

159. We hope that the reward is set"

160. Like this we pray before we eat

161. Then **Basmalah** to start the feast

162. First with dates or water if

163. There are no dates to start it with

164. When no water eat a sweet

165. But do not wait to start to eat

166. And if your fasting took a break

167. From sickness or from travels - sake

168. Then make it up some other day

169. And if you cant you gotta pay

NOTES

Chapter Ten

The Lineage of the Last Prophet

170. When asked about **rasoolullaah**

171. **Salla alayhi** from **Allaah**

172. Name **Ibraheem** and **Ismaaeel**

173. And only those we have **Daleel**

174. Like **Adnaan** and his son **Mudaar**

175. And **Fihrun** as the family star

176. For every **Fihrun's Qurayshee**

177. So all **Quraysh** must **Fihrun** be

178. **Ghaalib** ruled before **Lu-ayy**

179. And **Ka'b** spoke words that we still stay

180. **Murrah** was a household name

181. That many noble people claim

182. Like **Kilaab** and his son **Qusay**

183. Who son **Manaaf** had major say

184. Till **Haashim** came and crumbled bread

185. And gained respect from every head

186. And so did **Abdul Mutaalib**

187. Though **Shaybah** was the name he'd give

188. Then hundred camels **Abdullaah**

189. The father of **Rasoolullaah**

190. The messenger **Muhammadin**

191. **Salla alayhi wa sallam**

**Completed by the aid of Allaah
6 Shawwaal 1437
walHamdulillaah**

NOTES

NOTES

42935883R00020

Made in the USA
San Bernardino, CA
11 December 2016